Planet
Mercury

ANN O. SQUIRE

Children's Press®
An Imprint of Scholastic Inc.
New York Toronto London Auckland Sydney
Mexico City New Delhi Hong Kong
Danbury, Connecticut

Content Consultant
Bryan C. Dunne
Assistant Chair, Assistant Professor Department of Astronomy
University of Illinois at Urbana–Champaign
Urbana, Illinois

Library of Congress Cataloging-in-Publication Data
Squire, Ann.
 Mercury / Ann O. Squire.
 pages cm. — (A true book)
 Audience: Grade 4 to 6.
 Includes bibliographical references and index.
 ISBN 978-0-531-21153-3 (lib. bdg.) — ISBN 978-0-531-25359-5 (paperback)
 1. Mercury (Planet)—Juvenile literature. I. Title.
 QB611.S67 2014
 523.41—dc23   2013021639

All rights reserved. Published in 2014 by Children's Press, an imprint of Scholastic Inc.
Printed in China 62
SCHOLASTIC, CHILDREN'S PRESS, A TRUE BOOK™, and associated logos are trademarks and/or registered trademarks of Scholastic Inc.

1 2 3 4 5 6 7 8 9 10 R 23 22 21 20 19 18 17 16 15 14

**Front cover: The *MESSENGER*
spacecraft over Mercury**

**Back cover: Photo of Mercury,
taken by *MESSENGER***

Find the Truth!

Everything you are about to read is true *except* for one of the sentences on this page.

Which one is **TRUE**?

T or F The temperatures on Mercury are too extreme for humans to live there.

T or F There could once have been life on Mercury's moon.

Find the answers in this book.

Contents

THE **BIG** TRUTH!

Countless objects have impacted Mercury over time, creating the planet's many craters.

4 Exploring Mercury

How have spacecraft added to our understanding of Mercury? **39**

Ancient Greeks believed luck was a gift from the god Hermes, called Mercury by the Romans.

The colors in this image are enhanced to make it easier to see differences among rocks on Mercury's surface.

CHAPTER 1

A Hot, Dry Planet

Have you ever spent a summer day at the beach? If so, then you probably know how hot the sun can be. Sunglasses, sunblock, beach umbrellas, and dips in the ocean all help protect against the sun's burning rays. Now imagine that you lived on a **planet** more than twice as close to the sun as Earth is. The planet has almost no **atmosphere** to filter the sunlight. There is no water to cool you off. That's Mercury.

 Scientists did not know the length of Mercury's day until 1965.

Mercury in the Solar System

Mercury is one of the eight planets in our solar system that **orbit** the sun. Mercury is the planet closest to the sun. It is also the planet most affected by the sun's intense energy. Mercury is one of the four inner planets that are closest to the sun. The others are Venus, Earth, and Mars. Mercury is similar in many ways to the other inner planets. Unlike many planets, Mercury has no moons.

The planets, from nearest the sun, are Mercury, Venus, Earth, Mars, Jupiter, Saturn, Uranus, and Neptune. Pluto, a dwarf planet, is at the far edge of our solar system.

Sun Mercury Venus Earth Mars Jupiter Saturn Uranus Neptune

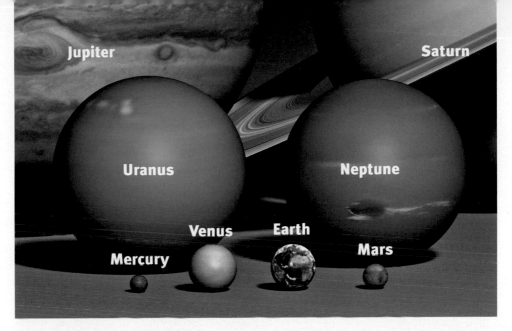

Jupiter

Saturn

Uranus

Neptune

Venus

Earth

Mercury

Mars

Gas giants such as Jupiter and Saturn are the largest planets in the solar system. Terrestrial planets are smaller.

Terrestrial Planet

Like the other inner planets, Mercury is **terrestrial**. It is composed of metal and rock. Its surface is hard and solid. The inner planets are much smaller than the outer ones. Mercury is the smallest of all. The planets farther from the sun are Jupiter, Saturn, Uranus, and Neptune. These planets are very different. They are much larger and are composed of gas or ice.

Mercury is just a little bigger than Earth's moon.

The Smallest Planet

Mercury measures only about 3,030 miles (4,876 kilometers) across. That is about the same as the distance across the United States. Mercury is less than half as wide as Earth. Its volume is much smaller. It would take 18 Mercurys to fill up Earth and more than 23 million Mercury's to fill up the sun. If the sun were the size of a tennis ball, Mercury would be a tiny speck of dust.

Distance From the Sun

Mercury's path around the sun is shaped like an oval, rather than a circle. Because of that, the distance between Mercury and the sun changes constantly and dramatically. The farthest point from the sun is called the aphelion. The closest is called the perihelion. Mercury's aphelion is 43 million miles (69 million km) from the sun. Its perihelion is 29 million miles (47 million km).

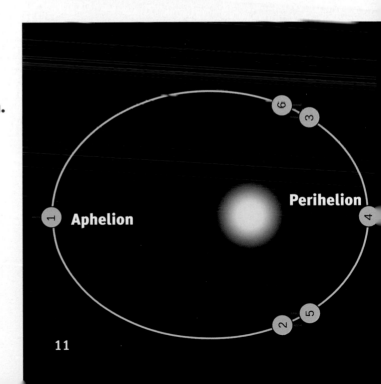

This illustration shows Mercury's orbit around the sun, marking where the planet is closest to and farthest from the sun.

1 Aphelion

Perihelion

Distance From Earth

Earth also orbits the sun. As it travels, its distance from Mercury ranges from 48 million miles (77 million km) to 138 million miles (222 million km). Mercury is closer to the sun than it is to Earth. As a result, Mercury always appears near the sun in Earth's sky. Because of the sun's brightness, Mercury is not visible during the daytime. The best times to spot it are early morning and early evening.

Mercury

Mercury rises and sets on Earth within about two hours of when the sun rises and sets.

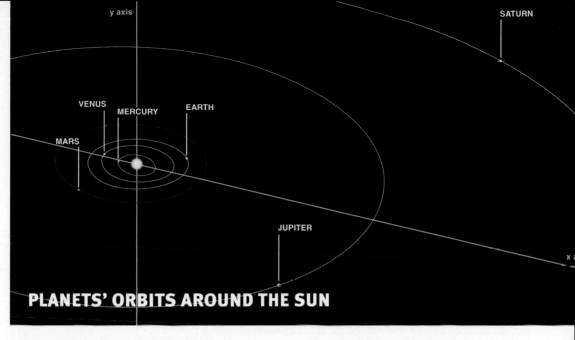

SATURN

VENUS

MERCURY

EARTH

MARS

JUPITER

x

PLANETS' ORBITS AROUND THE SUN

Mercury has the shortest trip around the sun of any planet in the solar system.

A Short Year

A year is the time it takes to complete one orbit around the sun. Mercury's year is shorter than any other planet's—only 88 of Earth's days. One reason for this is that Mercury is the fastest-moving planet in the solar system. It hurtles through space at an average of 30 miles (48 km) per second. Also, Mercury is very close to the sun. Its orbit is shorter than the distance traveled by planets farther away.

Mercury rotates only one and a half times during each of its orbits.

And a Long Day

If a year goes by quickly on Mercury, a day seems to take forever. Like other planets, Mercury rotates on its **axis**. This rotation creates a day on the planet. A day is the average time from one sunrise to the next sunrise. On Earth, a day is 24 hours long. Mercury's day is much longer. It lasts 176 of Earth's days. Earth has 365 days each Earth year. But the sun only rises on Mercury once every two Mercury years!

Why Mercury Has No Seasons

On Earth, we have four seasons: spring, summer, fall, and winter. The different seasons occur because Earth is tilted on its axis. When our North Pole is tilted toward the sun, the Northern Hemisphere experiences summer. When the North Pole is tilted away from the sun, it's winter in the Northern Hemisphere.

Mercury is hardly tilted at all. Mercury's north and south poles are always at the same angle to the sun, so there are no seasons.

CHAPTER 2

What Is Mercury Made Of?

Mercury is a rocky, metallic planet. Its huge **core** is probably made up of part solid and part **molten** Iron. Surrounding this is a thick layer of solid rock. On the outside is a thin, brittle crust. Mercury's surface looks gray and barren. It is covered with craters, valleys, and long, narrow ridges that look like wrinkles in the planet's surface.

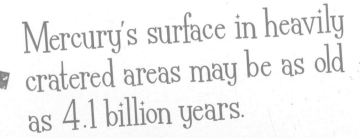
Mercury's surface in heavily cratered areas may be as old as 4.1 billion years.

A Dead Planet

Mercury was at one time **geologically** active, with a hot and turbulent core. Just as they did on Earth, volcanoes helped shape Mercury's surface. Now there is no sign of volcanic activity. **Astronomers** think that the core of Mercury cooled over time. This caused the planet to shrink slightly. When this happened, the crust thickened. Large wrinkles called scarps appeared. Because the crust is so thick and hard, no volcanic activity can reach the surface.

Mercury's crust may have bunched up into a series of ridges as the planet shrank.

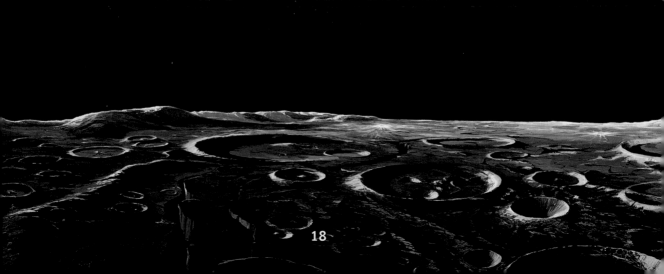

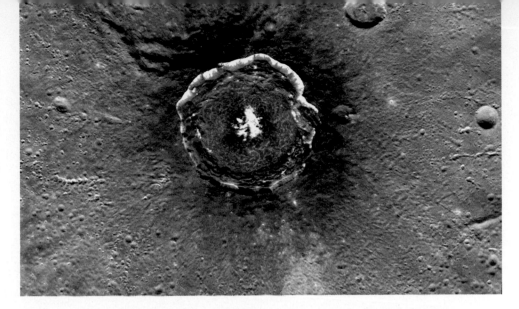

This crater, called Degas crater, has a high peak in the middle.

Covered With Craters

Mercury's surface is pockmarked with thousands of craters both large and small. They are called impact craters. That is because most were formed when **asteroids** and other objects crashed into Mercury's surface. These types of craters can also be seen on Earth. The largest known impact crater in the United States is beneath the Chesapeake Bay. It was created 35 million years ago when a large asteroid or **comet** crashed into Earth.

Craters on Mercury remain largely unchanged after they are created when asteroids or other objects hit.

Mercury has many more impact craters than Earth does. This is partly because Earth's thick atmosphere shields it against smaller objects from space. Asteroids approaching Earth are slowed and heated by our atmosphere. Most objects from space burn up before they reach the ground. When an asteroid does hit, erosion and other geologic activity wear down and cover the crater over time. Mercury has almost no atmosphere and no geologic activity. Therefore, more craters cover its surface.

Caloris Basin

The biggest impact crater on Mercury, and one of the biggest in the solar system, is the Caloris Basin. It measures 960 miles (1,545 km) across. Like other impact craters, it was formed when a huge asteroid or similar object struck the planet. The force of the collision was so great that it affected the opposite side of the planet. That region is now covered in hills that some scientists call the "weird terrain."

The colors in this photograph are enhanced to show differences across Mercury's surface. The Caloris Basin is the large orange area.

Crater Rays

Many astronomers have noticed bright streaks on Mercury's dull, gray surface. These are called crater rays. They are formed when an object hits the planet's surface. The impact crushes the rock beneath into a fine dust and sprays it in all directions. This crushed rock reflects light differently than the solid surface of the planet. As a result, it looks light and bright against the dark surface.

Crater rays can be bright when they are new. Generally, they fade over time.

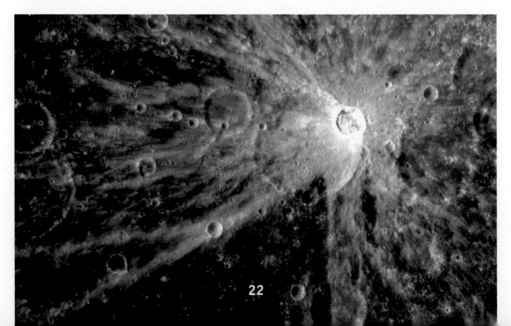

The solar wind blasts the part of Mercury facing the sun, blowing over the planet's surface and on into space.

Mercury's Atmosphere

Mercury has almost no atmosphere. Its surface gravity is only about one-third as strong as Earth's. This is not enough to hold atmospheric gases near the planet. In addition, Mercury is constantly bombarded by fast-moving winds from the sun. Even if Mercury's gravity could hold a thick atmosphere, this solar wind would blast it away. With no atmosphere, Mercury has no weather. There are no clouds, no rain, no fog—just a constant solar wind.

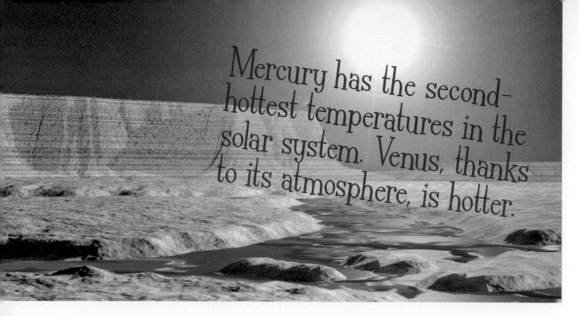

Mercury has the second-hottest temperatures in the solar system. Venus, thanks to its atmosphere, is hotter.

This illustration shows the sun as it appears from Mercury's surface.

Burning Hot

As the closest planet to the sun, Mercury has some of the highest temperatures of any planet in our solar system. During the day, it is extremely hot. It sometimes reaches more than 800 degrees Fahrenheit (427 degrees Celsius). The sun's rays are seven times stronger on Mercury than they are on Earth. If you stood on Mercury's surface, the sun would look more than twice as big across as it does on our planet.

And Freezing Cold

For a planet so close to the sun, you wouldn't think that Mercury could ever be cold. But there is no atmosphere to hold heat near the surface. Therefore, Mercury gets very, very cold at night. Nighttime temperatures can go down to nearly –300°F (–184°C). With temperatures that extreme, it is no wonder that life cannot exist on Mercury.

Temperatures drop rapidly as the sun sets on Mercury. There is no atmosphere to help the planet cool gradually, as on Earth.

Ice at the Poles

On a planet that gets as hot as Mercury does, the last thing you would expect to find is ice. But scientists believe that there is ice on Mercury. They suspect it is deep inside craters near the north and south poles. Even though Mercury is very close to the sun, its polar regions are always in the shadows. With no direct sunlight, any ice would stay permanently frozen.

Red areas in this image are places where no sunlight has been recorded. Yellow marks locations where ice has been detected.

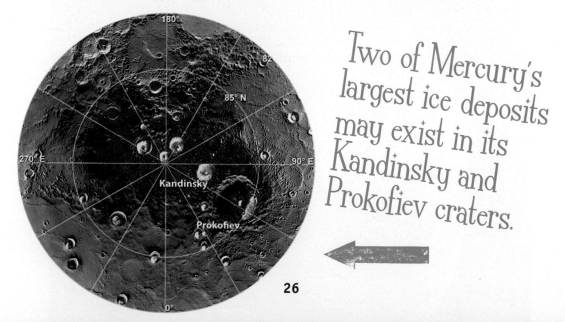

Two of Mercury's largest ice deposits may exist in its Kandinsky and Prokofiev craters.

Comets contain ice, which probably spreads across Mercury when a comet hits the planet.

Tons of Ice

Scientists think that there may be 100 billion to 1 trillion tons of frozen water at Mercury's poles. This is almost as much water as the amount contained in Lake Erie. But how did the water get there? The most likely source is comets. Comets create a cloud of water vapor when they strike Mercury. Some of this water vapor may get trapped at the poles and freeze into ice.

Strange Orbit

Mercury's orbit is highly elliptical, or oval-shaped. Also, the perihelion always falls at different points around the sun. For many years, scientists couldn't fully explain why.

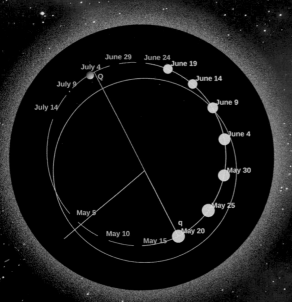

June 29 June 24 June 19
July 4 Q June 14
July 9 June 9
July 14 June 4
May 30
May 25
May 5 q May 20
May 10 May 15

The yellow and orange oval is Mercury's orbit in 2006. The gray circle would be a perfectly circular orbit centered on the sun.

Physicist Albert Einstein finally solved the puzzle. He determined that the sun's strong gravity actually curves the space and time around it.

Because Mercury is so close to the sun, its orbit is affected by this space-time curve.

A star bends space and time, shown by the grid, around it. This affects the path of the orbiting planet.

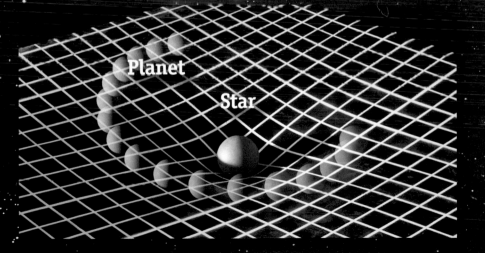

Planet

Star

Early Arab astronomers
study the night sky.

CHAPTER 3

Early Views of Mercury

Mercury, Mars, Jupiter, and other nearby planets can be seen without a telescope. Because of this, people have known about these planets since ancient times. It is impossible to say who originally discovered Mercury. It was described by the Sumerians as early as 3000 BCE, and by the Babylonians around 1400 BCE.

Babylonian astronomers recorded the positions of stars and planets over hundreds of years.

Two Planets or One?

Sometimes Mercury is visible in the early morning. At other times, it appears in the early evening. For many years, people believed that they were seeing two different planets. Greek astronomers named the morning planet Apollo and the evening planet Hermes. Not until the fourth century BCE did they realize that the morning and evening planets were one and the same.

Greek astronomers called the planets *asteres planetai*, or "wandering stars."

In the religion of ancient Rome, the god Mercury, like the Greek god Hermes, traveled quickly with the help of his winged sandals.

Messenger of the Gods

The Greek god Hermes was the messenger of the gods. Mercury is the name the Romans gave to the same god. That is the name we use for the planet today. Mercury was a swift-footed god. Many people think that the planet earned its name because it moves so quickly across the sky.

Some scholars have argued that ancient Romans thought that Woden was the same as the Roman god Mercury.

Wednesday's Planet

The ancient Greeks and Romans named the days of the week after gods and the objects in space that were known at the time. Mercury was the planet associated with Wednesday. Some of the names for Wednesday are *mercredi* in French, *mercoledì* in Italian, and *miércoles* in Spanish. Norse and Germanic peoples named this day after one of their main gods, Woden. In English, Woden's Day has become Wednesday.

Mercury Through a Telescope

In the early 1600s, Italian astronomer Galileo Galilei became one of the first to observe Mercury through a telescope. In 1639, an astronomer named Giovanni Battista Zupi discovered that Mercury showed phases like the moon. This could only be explained if Mercury orbited the sun. At the time, most people believed the sun, planets, and stars orbited Earth. But Mercury's phases supported a new idea that the sun was the center of the solar system.

Galileo built his first telescope in 1609.

35

The Limits of Hubble

The Hubble Space Telescope is a space-based telescope that orbits Earth. It sends back valuable information about the solar system. What can Hubble tell us about Mercury? Unfortunately, it cannot tell us anything. Mercury is too close to the sun. If Hubble tried to observe the planet, the sun's intense light would destroy the telescope's sensitive **optical** equipment.

The Hubble Space Telescope has been orbiting Earth since 1990.

Transits of
Mercury

Mercury's orbit lies between Earth and the sun.
From time to time, Earth, Mercury, and the sun
line up. Then it is possible to see Mercury passing
across the face of the sun as a small black dot. This
event is called a transit of Mercury. It occurs on
average 13 times each century, usually in November
or May. The most recent Mercury transit was in
November 2006. The next will occur in May 2016.

The Sun

Mercury

38

CHAPTER 4

Exploring Mercury

Mercury is a very difficult planet to study through telescopes or with spacecraft. Being so close to the sun and its strong gravity means that it takes a lot of energy for a spacecraft to reach Mercury without being pulled toward the sun. Astronomers estimate that sending a spacecraft straight to Mercury uses more rocket fuel than a trip in the other direction to the edge of our solar system!

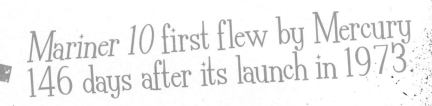

Mariner 10 first flew by Mercury 146 days after its launch in 1973.

Mariner 10

Mariner 10 was launched in 1973. It was the first spacecraft sent to study Mercury. After passing Venus, *Mariner 10* arrived at Mercury early in 1974. The craft flew past the planet three times over the course of a year. The spacecraft sent back the first photos of Mercury's cratered surface. As it passed, *Mariner 10* discovered a weak magnetic field on Mercury. It also measured the planet's daytime and nighttime temperatures.

Timeline of Mercury Exploration

1965
Astronomers discover the length of Mercury's day.

1631
Astronomer Pierre Gassendi makes the first observation of a transit of Mercury.

1974
Mariner 10 is the first spacecraft to fly past Mercury.

MESSENGER

In 2004, National Aeronautics and Space Administration (NASA) scientists launched the *MESSENGER* spacecraft. Over the next seven years, *MESSENGER* flew by Mercury several times, as well as by Earth and Venus. In 2011, it began to orbit Mercury. As of 2013, it was still doing so. During its orbit, *MESSENGER* comes very close to Mercury's surface. The spacecraft is equipped with insulation and a huge sunshade to protect it from the sun's intense rays.

2004
NASA launches *MESSENGER* on a mission to Mercury.

2011
MESSENGER goes into orbit around Mercury.

1991
Scientists find the first evidence of ice at Mercury's polar regions.

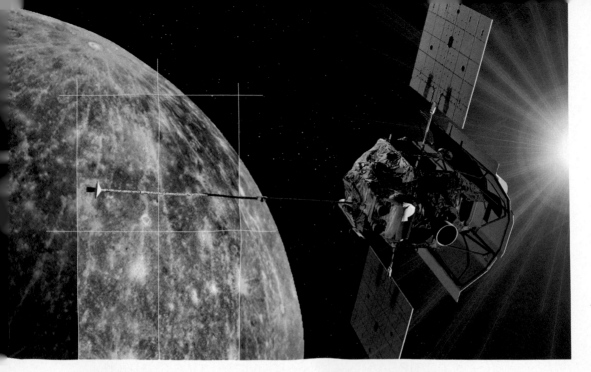

MESSENGER has mapped the entire planet in enhanced colors.

MESSENGER has made some surprising discoveries. It had revealed that the planet's metallic core is much larger than scientists thought. It found ice in craters at Mercury's poles. Most surprising of all, MESSENGER found a layer of tarlike, **organic** material in the polar craters. This material was not produced from living matter. But it does contain carbon and hydrogen, two ments that are essential for life.

BepiColombo

A third mission to Mercury is still in the planning stages. The mission is called BepiColombo. The European Space Agency (ESA) and the Japan Aerospace Exploration Agency (JAXA) hope to launch twin orbiters. One spacecraft will study the surface and internal structure of Mercury. The other will gather information about Mercury's magnetic field. Mercury is still the least-known planet, but we are learning more about it every day. ★

One of the BepiColombo orbiters will have a highly elliptical orbit as it studies Mercury's magnetic field.

True Statistics

Number of Mercurys that could fit inside planet Earth: 18

Distance traveled by *MESSENGER* before going into orbit around Mercury: 4.9 billion miles (7.9 billion km)

Weight of a 100 lb. (45 kg) person on Mercury: 38 lb. (would feel like 17.2 kg on Earth)

Number of moons orbiting Mercury: 0

Thickness of Mercury's outer layer, or crust: 300 to 400 mi. (483 to 644 km)

Temperature difference between night and day on Mercury: 1,080°F (600°C)

Did you find the truth?

(T) The temperatures on Mercury are too extreme for humans to live there.

(F) There could once have been life on Mercury's moon.

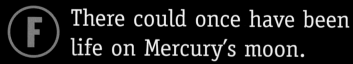

Resources

Books

Aguilar, David A. *13 Planets: The Latest View of the Solar System*. Washington, DC: National Geographic, 2011.

Arlon, Penelope, and Tory Gordon-Harris. *Planets*. New York: Scholastic, 2012.

Owen, Ruth. *Mercury*. New York: Windmill Books, 2014.

Visit this Scholastic Web site for more information on Mercury:
★ www.factsfornow.scholastic.com
Enter the keyword **Mercury**

Important Words

asteroids (AS-tuh-roidz) — small, rocky objects that travel around the sun

astronomers (uh-STRAH-nuh-muhrz) — scientists who study stars, planets, and space

atmosphere (AT-muhs-feer) — the mixture of gases that surrounds a planet

axis (AK-sis) — an imaginary line through the middle of an object, around which that object spins

comet (KAH-mit) — a bright body in space that has a long tail of light

core (KOR) — the most inner part of a planet

geologically (jee-uh-LAH-jih-klee) — having to do with a planet's physical structure

molten (MOHL-tuhn) — melted at a high temperature, usually describing metal or rock

optical (AHP-ti-kuhl) — having to do with eyes or eyesight, or related to light

orbit (OR-bit) — to travel in a path around something, especially a planet or the sun

organic (or-GAN-ik) — containing carbon and hydrogen

planet (PLAN-it) — a large body orbiting a star

terrestrial (tuh-RES-tree-uhl) — relating to land as distinct from air or water

Index

Page numbers in **bold** indicate illustrations

About the Author

Ann O. Squire is a psychologist and an animal behaviorist. Before becoming a writer, she studied the behaviors of rats, tropical fish in the Caribbean, and electric fish from central Africa. Her favorite part of being a writer is the chance to learn as much as she can about all sorts of topics. In addition to *Mars*, *Jupiter*, *Mercury*, *Neptune*, and *Saturn*, Dr. Squire has written about many different animals, from lemmings to leopards and cicadas to cheetahs. She lives in Long Island City, New York.